SELF-DEVELOPMENT

THE CAREER SKILLS LIBRARY

Communication Skills
By Richard Worth

Information Management
By Joe Mackall

Leadership Skills
By Diane E. Rossiter

Learning the Ropes
By Sharon Naylor

Organization Skills
By Richard Worth

Problem-Solving
By Dandi Daley Mackall

Self-Development
By Dandi Daley Mackall

Teamwork Skills
By Dandi Daley Mackall

SELF-DEVELOPMENT

by Dandi Daley Mackall

A New England Publishing Associates Book

Copyright ©1998 by Ferguson Publishing Company, Chicago, Illinois

Printed in the United States of America
U-8

Library of Congress Cataloging-in-Publication Data

Mackall, Dandi Daley.
    Self-development / by Dandi Daley Mackall.
        p.   cm.
    Includes bibliographical references and index.
    ISBN 0-89434-214-2
    1. Vocational guidance. 2. Career development. 3. Job
    satisfaction. 4. Highschool graduates—Employment. 5. Personality
    and occupation. 6. Work ethic. I. Title. II. Series.
    HF5381.M196   1998
    650.1—dc21   97-28448
                                     CIP

CONTENTS

INTRODUCTION

From coast to coast, employers search for the ideal employee. Skills and experience count, but most businesses are looking for something else, too. Character.

The kind of person you are matters to your employer.

One of the most important things you can do right now for your career is to develop the character qualities employers want. How responsible are you? Are you the kind of person others count on? Have you developed good habits like working hard, striving for excellence, acting like a professional? It's never too early or too late for self-development.

Great management is about character, not technique.

**—Thomas Teal,
Harvard Business Review**

This book begins with your favorite subject—*you*. You'll unlock the secrets of your temperament, your learning style, your strengths and weaknesses, your values. Then we'll take an honest look at what employers want to see in you when you show up for

(Courtesy: Prints & Photographs Division, Library of Congress)

When billionaire John D. Rockefeller hired young
people, he focused on the quality of their characters.

work. In the end, you'll get tips from how to manage your time to how you can impress almost anyone with your amazing memory.

So relax. Read. You're about to discover that your best secret weapon to a successful career could be *you.*

The most important thing for a young
man [woman] is to establish a credit—
a reputation, character.

—John D. Rockefeller

CHAPTER ONE
WHO ME?

What's your favorite topic of conversation? Probably the answer is you. Most of us spend more time thinking, worrying, and dreaming about ourselves than we spend on all other subjects combined.

But how well do you really know yourself?

Self-knowledge is in. People pay analysts thousands of dollars to learn more about themselves. We read books on self-image and self-improvement. We listen to radio psychologists and we talk with friends.

What does all this have to do with your career? Plenty. Remember: character counts.

If you're just beginning your career, in a way, you're on the verge of becoming a whole new person. Talk to people who have recently graduated and started careers. Most of them will have stories of how much they've changed because of their work environments.

Michele got a first-year teaching job as a coach at a state special education school. As she talks about her experiences, she shakes her head, still amazed at what she learned about herself. "I thought I was pretty together. But I didn't have a clue how I'd react to so much responsibility. Nothing in school prepared me for being in charge of so much. I kind of thought I was outgoing, but all I wanted to do was retreat—hide out."

Ben discovered new things about himself when he joined a group of trainees as part of a telecommunications company. He admits, "I would have said I was pretty mature. But three months of training really threw me. I didn't think I was an emotional person, but I went up and down, highs and lows—all over the emotional map. I didn't know what was going on."

Be more concerned with your character than your reputation, because your character is what you really are, while your reputation is merely what others think you are.
—John Wooden

Meredith took a job as part of a secretarial pool in a large investment firm. She started getting depressed her first week at work. Everybody else seemed outgoing and excited about the new challenges. Meredith dreaded every change. Then she remembered some of the material she'd read on personality types.

"In one of my classes, we took personality tests. I came out the type who is reliable, but doesn't like new things. So I knew that what may have come naturally for my coworkers just didn't for me. But that was okay. I could do what I needed to socially. At the same time, I could make myself indispensable by using my strengths. I didn't have to try to imitate their strengths."

KNOW YOURSELF

Now is the right time for you to get to know yourself. Self-knowledge won't make all the surprises and stresses of your first year on the job go away. But you'll be better prepared for those changes and better able to understand your own reactions.

Self-knowledge won't make all the surprises and stresses of your first year on the job go away.

If you can learn more about yourself, you can equip yourself for your career. For example, if you know that your energy can only get "refueled" when you're alone, you know to plan time to be by yourself. If you're aware of your laid-back tendencies, you know to give yourself an occasional go-ahead kick.

Knowing yourself gives you a chance to meet your own needs. That takes pressure off at work. Then, if your job doesn't meet your expectations, your whole world won't fall apart.

FACTOID:

Noted psychologist, Carl R. Rogers, claims self-discovery is the basis of psychological health and success. From treating thousands of patients, he concludes that one central issue lies behind almost every problem—the lack of self-knowledge.

PROFILES AND TYPES

You may mean many things when you say someone has a great personality. And when you refer to someone who's "not your type," you may mean something entirely different. But psychologists generally refer to personality and type by certain categories. Many of these categories are based on opposite characteristics: introvert/extrovert; feeling/thinking; perceiving/judging; sensing/intuiting.

People seem to be born with tendencies toward different temperaments, learning styles, and thinking styles. No one style is the right one, or even the preferable one. But if you know your styles and your temperament, you can use your strengths in work situations—and be on guard against your potential weaknesses.

> People seem to be born with tendencies toward different temperaments, learning styles, and thinking styles.

PERSONALITY

Personality. Everybody has one. In the ninth century, an Arab physician divided the personalities of temperaments into four categories: phlegmatic, sanguine, choleric, and melancholy. Many variations exist, and nobody fits completely into one of the categories. Yet most of us can easily see ourselves in one or two of these four divisions.

The following exercise is a personality inventory to give you clues as you investigate who you are. The exercise is designed to give you an idea about personality...and to entertain. For more accurate information, and a much more thorough inventory, ask your school counselor to give you the Meyer-Briggs Type Indicator or any of the more scientific inventories your school recommends.

EXERCISE

Four categories of
personality traits are given
in the chart below. Divide
a sheet of paper into four
quarters. Mark one quarter
with a P at the top, one with
an S, one with a C and one
with an M. Under each
letter, write the words
or phrases from the
corresponding quarters of
the chart that describe you
most of the time. (Please
don't write in a library
book—it's a sign of bad
character!)

PHLEGMATIC

easygoing
discerning
uninvolved
not bossy
consistent
a spectator
stubborn
accurate
detailed
pleasant
submissive
rarely angry
dry humor
kindhearted
indecisive
orderly
calm
adjusts well
reserved
steady
can be lazy
can imitate others
fearful
predictable
laid-back
factual
timid
sleepy
scheduled
peacemaker
analytical
controlled

SANGUINE	CHOLERIC	MELANCHOLY
laughs a lot	domineering	analytical
conceited	impudent	creative
optimistic	logical	moody
enthusiastic	active	shy
inspirational	confident	visionary
friendly	controlled	pessimistic
poor listener	poor listener	gIfted
dislikes being alone	enterprising	hypochondria
likes new things	purposeful	genius tendencies
bubbly	hard to discourage	self-sacrificing
verbal	determined	individualistic
likes taking risks	quarrelsome	intense
spontaneous	angry	suspicious
fun-loving	decisive	self-centered
popular	inflexible	critical
lacks follow-	ambitious	fearful
through	goal-oriented	private
outgoing	good planner	may be depressed
pleasant	problem solver	perfectionist
adventurous	handles pressure well	emotional
initiator	leader	faithful friend
makes others laugh	demanding	thinks"too much"
likes change	strong-willed	sensitive
gets bored easily	likes a challenge	vengeful
shallow	impatient	sad
relationships	pushy	gets feelings hurt
angry	well-organized	artsy
smiles a lot	self-reliant	introvert
visionary	opinionated	dependable
motivator	hot-tempered	slow to initiate
energetic	practical	bashful
talkative	independent	feels guilty
forgets easily	competitive	solitary
	insensitive	imaginative
	stubborn	
	firm	
	adventurous	
	brave	

APPLYING YOUR KNOWLEDGE OF PERSONALITY

Look over your sheet. Does one personality type predominate? To get another perspective, ask a parent, sibling, or friend to do this inventory according to their perception of you. These inventories are designed to get you thinking about your personality type. For more detailed analysis, ask your guidance counselor.

Each of the four temperaments, or personality types, carries with it a set of strengths and corresponding weaknesses. If you wrote most of your words and phrases under one category, pay special attention to the tendencies of that temperament.

Phlegmatic

The phlegmatic may need to be on guard against laziness.

Life for the phlegmatic-type person tends to go along smoothly. Her strengths lie in her combination of abilities and her steady consistency. She can relax, enjoy friends, and keep the peace. She's easy to live with and undemanding. The phlegmatic may need to be on guard against laziness or a lack of motivation that keeps her on the sidelines as a spectator. She can become stubborn, indecisive, and even fearful.

Melancholy

The melancholic-type person sees things in life that others miss. He's sensitive and often gifted. He doesn't mind sacrificing himself for others and makes a faithful friend, a good listener, thoughtful of others. His perfectionist tendencies make him conscious of letting people down.

The melancholic may need to work on controlling his moods, which can vary widely with his emotions. He needs to stand up for himself. He may have to work on meeting new people and not worrying what others think about him.

Sanguine

A sanguine temperament is great in a crowd. He loves new situations and experiences, and is seldom at a loss for words. He's cheerful, enthusiastic and a great motivator, full of energy. The sanguine person may need to improve his organization and follow-through. He should work on becoming a better listener and on forming deeper relationships. Sanguines tend to get bored easily and become restless and undisciplined.

Choleric

The choleric is independent, decisive, and self-sufficient. She makes decisions easily and usually is a strong leader. She loves activity, has lots of ideas, and the plans to implement them. She's determined, practical, and she knows her own mind.

The choleric may be so goal-oriented, she'll need to be careful not to overlook other people's needs. She can be a tough person to live with, inflexible, and impatient. She may need to work on people skills to become a motivator rather than a dictator.

LEARNING STYLES

You've probably heard about recent studies on how our brains function. Basically, the brain has two sides and each hemisphere functions differently. Most of us depend more on one side of the brain than the other as we learn new information. In part, that explains our different learning styles.

For example, you want to give your little sister a tricycle for Christmas. Christmas Eve comes, and it's time to assemble the pieces. Do you pull out the instruction book and read through it step-by-step? Or do you dump everything out on the living room carpet and start figuring what goes where? What you do has a lot to say about your learning style.

Some of us are more "left-brained," or analytical in

(Joe Duffy)

"Not only did I do it without instructions, but look at all the spare parts I have left over!"

the way we learn. Give us the instruction book and well-ordered steps. The left side of the brain handles numbers, words, details. It's organized, sequential. The left brain analyzes parts.

"Right-brained" people see the whole picture. They remember faces (forget the names), patterns, images. Give them a vision of what's needed, and let them create, spontaneously. They'll get that tricycle together eventually. Forget the instruction book.

19

BRAIN HEMISPHERE DOMINANCE

LEFT-BRAIN LEARNER	RIGHT-BRAIN LEARNER
Sees in parts	Sees the whole
Logical	Creative
Learns in numbered steps	Learns by figuring out
Follows in straight line	Sees the pattern
Likes words	Likes images
Orderly, organized	Spontaneous

Another difference in learning style is whether we learn more effectively through hearing (auditory), seeing and writing (visual), or touching (kinesthetic). The auditory learner learns best from word of mouth. Verbal instruction has the most impact—hearing someone's name, listening to instructions.

The visual learner tends to think in pictures and remember what she sees or writes. Hearing directions doesn't work as well as reading those directions.

A kinesthetic learner prefers to learn by doing. Reading or hearing isn't as effective for him as hands-on instruction. Touch is important to the learning process.

APPLYING YOUR KNOWLEDGE OF LEARNING STYLES

Just think about the way you learn best in class. Does it help you to write and rewrite dates or words in order to learn them? Or are you better off saying them aloud? Do you remember more by listening intently to your teacher (auditory), or by taking notes, or reading the information (visual)? Do flash cards, finger spelling, hands-on learning activities help you remember and learn (kinesthetic)?

Understanding your learning style can make a smoother transition to your new job. Imagine your first week on the job. How can you learn and remember names, duties, operations, procedures? If you're a visual learner, it may help to carry around a notebook and record new information and names. Auditory learners can discuss procedures and repeat names aloud. Kinesthetic learners could practice new procedures immediately or take notes and make their own study sheets later. They can look for hands-on tutorials.

If you're a left-brain learner, you may want to organize your own steps for new procedures. If you're a right-brain learner, write down names to go with the faces you remember.

Pay attention to what works for you now in your

Understanding your learning style can make a smoother transition to your new job.

classes. Then be ready to make the most out of your learning style when you start your career.

INTROVERTS AND EXTROVERTS

You may already feel you know whether you're an extrovert or an introvert. In general, extroverts are outgoing, like the sanguine personality type. They're good in a crowd and enjoy meeting new people. Extroverts tend to be talkers and doers, looking for the action, thriving on activity.

Introverts are thought to be quieter, more private people. They may be shy, more comfortable with the familiar. They enjoy deep friendships and the company of a few good friends. But crowds make them uncomfortable and they retreat.

Still, recent studies have pointed out a significant difference in the categories. Some people may simply be good at faking extroversion, even to themselves. They have mastered speech and verbal skills and the art of storytelling. All these qualities lead them to believe they are extroverts.

But the truth is, some of these supposed extroverts are in reality introverts. They're just good performers. A more reliable indicator may be your answer to this question: How do you refuel your energy? When you're with a crowd all day or night, do you become energized, an energy that takes you into the next day? If so, you are probably the extrovert you believed yourself to be.

Or, even though you handle yourself well in a crowd, do you only refuel when you're alone? Do you need to get off by yourself to get your head together or get your energy back? Then you are probably more of an introvert who has learned to be good in a crowd.

What difference does it make whether you're an introvert or an extrovert? Neither is better. But if you understand yourself, you can help yourself ease into your new job. For example, if you're an introvert, take some of your breaks or lunches alone. Use your time at home to refuel. Recognize your need for that alone-time and schedule it in.

If you're an extrovert, volunteer for speaking assignments or events where you can use your social skills. But be careful to use those social skills wisely. It's up to you to monitor your enthusiasm and share the spotlight. You'll want to check yourself in meetings to make sure you don't talk too much.

It helps to know yourself.

EXERCISE

1. For each type or category below, write down where you see yourself. In a sentence or two, explain your choice.

   A. Temperament: (phlegmatic, sanguine, choleric, melancholy)

   B. Learning style: (left-brain, right-brain)

   C. Learning style: (auditory, visual, kinesthetic)

   D. Social: (introvert, extrovert)

2. Take a minute and compile a list of strengths and weaknesses.

	STRENGTHS	WEAKNESSES
By myself	content	lazy
	organized	easily bored
With others	make friends easily	don't speak up
	can make others laugh	too critical
At work/ school	make Bs	should make As
	consistent	don't work hard
Skills/talents	music	math
	writing	mechanical
Miscellaneous	lots of ideas	messy

You should come up with many more strengths and weaknesses than appear here in this example. Get input from friends, family, teachers—anyone who might help you get a clearer understanding of yourself. For each weakness, ask yourself if the flip side might be a strength. For example, if you have trouble making friends (weakness), are you a faithful friend to the ones you have (strength)?

2

WHY ME? (VALUES AND ETHICS)

Juanita had been working as an editorial assistant for just two hours when she faced her first ethical dilemma. Her boss asked her to lie. "If anyone calls for me," he said, "tell them I've left for the day. I've got to get caught up on work."

Juanita had always thought of herself as an honest person. How could she lie? On the other hand, she'd only been on the job two hours. How could she challenge her boss? What would you do if you were Juanita?

WHAT'S IMPORTANT

Few of us know consciously what we subconsciously value. Values are those things and principles that are most important to us. Values involve our feelings, ideas, and beliefs. Whether you're aware of it or not, you operate according to a system of values. Everything you do, every decision you make, comes from inside you—from your own (conscious or unconscious) system of values.

Should I drop out of Advanced English?

Yes. My social life is too important to spend that much time reading. This is my senior year and I don't want to miss out on time with my friends. I can't pass that course without cutting back on TV. That course would lower my grade point average and maybe I couldn't play basketball.

No. I need the course for college. I like literature. My best friend is taking that class. Everybody who's going on to college will take it, and I don't want kids to think I'm not. My parents will flip if I don't take the course.

You make choices all day and probably never stop to think about your values. But your values are at work just the same. At school, you're used to the possibilities and consequences of most choices. But what about when you start a new career? How will you know what to choose when, like Juanita, you face a tough decision?

Now is the time to get a handle on your values. Know yourself well. Then, when you have to choose, you'll have a better understanding of what's at stake. When Juanita's boss told her to lie and say he was out

(V. Harlow/Russell Library)

During the course of your career, you'll be asked to make some difficult ethical choices. If you have a clear sense of what's right and what's wrong, making the correct decision will be much easier. Sometimes you may have to pay a price for doing "the right thing." In the end, however, the price you will pay for violating your own conscience will be far higher.

of the office, she panicked. Many receptionists and assistants have faced that situation with an "Okay, Boss." They hardly gave it a thought.

But Juanita knew herself well enough to understand she could not just say "okay." Juanita's parents and her personal faith had instilled honesty as one of the highest values. Trembling, she asked to talk with her employer. Instead of telling him she didn't want to lie for him, Juanita offered an alternative she could live with.

She explains what happened next. "I said, 'Mr. _____, would it be all right if I told callers you couldn't come to the phone or that you were unavailable and could I take a message?' He looked at me a moment, and I wondered if I'd have the shortest employment on record. Then he said, 'Sure, that's fine.' And that was that."

Clearly defined values will aid you in everything you do. In an important sense, your crystallized values serve as banisters on a staircase, to guide you, to be touched when you have to make decisions, and in very risky matters, grasped.
—Eugene Raudsepp,
Growth Games for the Creative Manager

Ideally, in your career, you'll make decisions according to your values. But if you're not aware of your own values, you can expect confusion. A good knowledge of personal values will help you take responsibility for your decisions and your career.

Observing Yourself

How well do you know yourself on the inside? Do you make your decisions according to what you think is most important? Do you think you're unselfish, polite, respectful, generous, honest?

Try this. Start a journal of self-observations. For one week, see what you can discover about your values. Observe yourself and the reactions you get from others. Pay attention to the value system that's at work in everything you do. It may or may not match the values you think you have. The more you know about yourself—on the inside—the more control you can have over your value system.

EXERCISE

One way to understand your personal values is self-assessment. Ask your guidance counselor to give you a values clarification assessment. In the meantime, photocopy the values quiz on pages 31 and 32 and try your hand at it.

One Student's Self-Observation Journal:

Monday—

I noticed I only said hi to four kids before class, and I know all of them well. Unfriendly? I made sure I greeted Kevin because he's the leader, the most popular in our class. I guess it's important to me to be popular too.

Mrs. H., my English teacher likes me. Only class I voluntarily choose the front-row seat. Why? I do want to go to college. That's important to me. Her class could make a difference in how I do. Plus, she's friends with my mom. I value what Mom thinks about me, although I wouldn't admit it to anybody, especially Mrs. H....or Mom.

Seems I always make W. mad. Why? Ask her? I value our friendship. That's important to me. But it doesn't keep me from talking about her to Kevin. Does that mean I value his popularity more than her friendship? That's worth considering.

T. talks to me about everything, like I'm easy to talk to. Wonder why? What signals do I give off? I'll ask. Helping people by listening is important to me. I'll tell them whatever I think will make them feel good. That's more important than absolutely being honest and telling T. to lose 15 lbs.

Rode home with J. and K. Lots of laughs. We always go where K. wants to. I wanted to head for Wendy's, but didn't say so. Put off studying for history test until almost 10:00 P.M. Kept falling asleep. I don't know whether to read my notes or study the chapter. I should have asked, should have taken better notes, should have started earlier. Maybe I need to make a study schedule and keep it—if college is so important to me.

Values Quiz

For each item on the following pages, mark how important you think it is to you. If you're not sure, ask yourself, "Would I drive 200 miles for this (to go to church, visit a friend, vote)?"

	Very Important	Important	Somewhat	Unimportant
God	X			
Church			X	
Family		X		
Doing my best	X			
Friends		X		
Grades				X
Being sensitive to the feelings of others			X	
Sports/extracurricular activities			X	
School				X
Independence	X			
Winning			X	
Economic security		X		
Inner peace	X			
Adventure		X		
Serving others				X
My country			X	

(Continued on the next page)

31

(Values Quiz continued)

	Very Important	Important	Somewhat	Unimportant
Status			X	
Respect from others	X			
Self-respect	X			
Fun		X		
Honesty	X			
Home		X		
Money		X		
Prestige	X			
Fame				X
TV				X
Dating			X	
Sex				X
Possessions				X
Hobbies		X		
What others think of me				X
The arts			X	
Popularity				X
Health	X			
Compassion	X			
Excellence	X			
Love	X			

Now, evaluate those items you've indicated as very important. Ask yourself how many of your decisions and daily actions reflect your values. Do the same for the items you consider unimportant. How much do your values affect your lifestyle?

9/10

VALUE QUESTIONS

Another way to get at the root of your values is to ask yourself questions. Remember, the more you understand your own values, the better equipped you'll be to handle the tough choices in a new career.

Take a few minutes to answer these questions as honestly as you can:

What are my dreams? *To Be Holy/Go to Heaven*

Who are my mentors or idols? *Jesus, God, Mom, me*

Of what things am I proudest physically, mentally, emotionally? *P = energy Lvls, m = High IQ E = empathy*

in connection with my family? *Yes, sorta*

at school? *No*

a talent? *many Talents*

with my hands? *Yes, I'm Handy!*

verbally? *I Have High charisma*

something nobody knows but me? *I'm Special*

What do I want most out of life?

Respect.

Complete the following:

At least I'm somebody who ... *Cares*

People disagree, but I think ... *God's Real*

Secretly, I wish ... *To Be Rich*

If I had one week to live, I'd ... *Do Drugs*

If I got a million dollars, I'd ... *Be Happy*

Nobody can change my mind about ... *Jesus*

By the time I'm 65, I want to ... *Have wife, Have Kids*

Define yourself in four words: "I am *Smart*, *Athletic*, *Lucky*, and *Brave*."

Define who you want to be in four words: "I wish I were *Stronger*, *Taller*, *Tougher*, and *more Awesome*."

My personal motto could be:

Three things I could never live without are: *God Lord / Jesus*, *Food/water*, and *Sleep*.

Now sit back and examine your answers. Did you learn anything about yourself? Would your friends be surprised at any of your answers? Are you?

Know yourself and your values. They should form the basis for goals, decisions, and actions.

Most important to you above everything else are your integrity and personal values. You always can lose a job and get another one. You always can lose money and make more. But once you compromise your integrity and personal values, they can never be regained.
—**Tom Fischgrund,**
*The Insider's Guide to the
Top-20 Careers in Business and Management*

ETHICS

Ethics is a system or code of morals. Once you know your values and what's important to you, ethics can help you set goals and achieve what you want without breaking your own set of unwritten rules of life.

"Ethics" comes from the Greek word *ethos*, meaning "character."

Ethics deals with right and wrong. In a way, it's the code of unwritten rules about how we act toward others. In fact, "ethics" comes from the Greek word ethos, meaning "character." Socrates, the great fifth-century B.C. Greek philosopher, asked his students to ask themselves this question: "Why do you do what you do?"

Values are the things we consider important. Ethics are the "shoulds" and "should nots" of living as we try to get what we want.

THOU SHALT...AND THOU SHALT NOT

When Juanita's boss asked her to lie for him, Juanita experienced a personal, ethical conflict. She wanted to succeed in her career. She wanted to please her boss. But somewhere inside her, she heard a voice: "Thou shalt not lie, Juanita." And she had an ethical dilemma.

Few of us will ever know exactly where we got all our ideas of moral shoulds and should nots. Much of our ethical make up comes from our parents, families, peers, and our religion or belief system.

Act so that you can simultaneously will that the maxim of your action should become universal law.
                    —**Immanuel Kant, 18th-century**
                              German philosopher
[In other words, don't do anything unless you would want everybody else to do the same thing in your place.]

Imagine yourself in these situations and think about what you would do.

- You are part of a public relations campaign designed to sell widgets. You know that your company's product isn't as good as your competitor's product. Yet you're expected to create

(Courtesy: Prints & Photographs Division, Library of Congress)

During the 18th century, German philosopher Immanuel Kant developed a sound and common-sense guideline for moral behavior: Do as you would have others do. You can't go wrong if you follow this principle.

slogans making false claims about your widget's superiority. What would you do?

Christine found herself in this situation (though not over widgets). She values honesty and integrity, but she also values her own creativity...and her job. Her decision was to go all out on the campaign. She refrained from quoting false statistics or creating mythical testimonials. But she did make general claims, false claims, that their product tastes better and is more popular than the competition. Although Christine wasn't 100% satisfied with her decision, she feels she made the best decision she could.

Other people have chosen to resign or asked to be released from a campaign they didn't feel they could endorse. Think about ethical issues now, so you won't be completely surprised later.

- A customer comes to you with a valid complaint. You know her complaint is valid because you've heard it from many others this month. Company policy, however, is to deny wrongdoing because of the store's no-return policy. How will you handle this customer?

Travis and Sandra work for a company with a similar no-return policy. They've handled this situation in different ways, according to their individual ethical codes. Travis follows the company's advice to the letter. He believes what his boss does is up to him. He took the job and owes the store his loyalty. Because of his personal ambition and loyalty to his boss, Travis never tells the customer that the product is probably defective.

Sandra is very involved in her local synagogue. Most of her personal ethics come from her faith. Since she can't reconcile the "silent deceit" of not being completely honest with the customer, Sandra often tells the customer that other products like hers have been returned. She even advises the customer not to purchase the same brand again. Sandra explained her decision to her boss. As long as the company doesn't suffer from Sandra's honesty, the boss has agreed to let her handle customers this way. Sandra says if she's told not to be honest, she's prepared to look for a new job.

F A C T O I D :

When Barbara Dafoe Whitehead, research associate at the Institute for American Values, asked parents what their basic responsibility was, the number one answer was: "Teaching my kids right from wrong."

YOUR PERSONAL CODE OF ETHICS

Become familiar with your own, code of ethics. Understanding your "unwritten rules" will help you make decisions you can live with.

You make ethical decisions every day. Ask yourself why you do what you do.

Do you cheat on tests? What unwritten rules influence your decision?

Would you try to date your best friend's steady? It's not illegal. So why or why not?

Would you smoke a cigarette or a joint if you were positive you wouldn't get caught? Virtue is going beyond what you're legally bound to.

Would you gossip about a friend? an acquaintance? an enemy? Does your answer change? Why?

Would you tell a white lie to a teacher or parent if it saved you from a hassle?

Would you tell a white lie if it saved someone's feelings?

Examine your decisions. See if you can decipher your own ethical code. Is it the way you want it to be? If not, now's the time to start changing it—before you hit the pressures of a new career.

EXERCISE

1. If your house were on fire, what ten items would you try to rescue?

Pets, money, Clothes, TV, Food, XBox, PHone, Wallet, SHoes, meditation, Bizykle

2. Write five bumper sticker slogans you wouldn't mind sticking on your car.

I Love Jesus!
Go - Blue! ~~team~~ UM, wolverines!
I Need pizza!
God Bless America
belreve in yourself
I Know Karate

3. Your corporation is secretly dumping toxic materials into the river that runs through your city. Will you do anything about it? If so, what? What values and ethics come into play in your decision?

yes!

I wtll tell Athorities about this. I will expose them.

41

3 CHAPTER THREE
DEPENDABILITY (SOMEBODY TO COUNT ON)

In a recent survey, employers were asked: "What's the one quality you look for more than any other in a would-be employee?" Over three-quarters responded, "Dependability or responsibility." Want to make the "Most Wanted" business bulletin board? Be the kind of person on whom others can depend.

THE BASICS

If nothing is more important than dependability to your employer, how do you prove you're dependable? Obviously, you have to be dependable (show up on time, get your work done). If you don't come through on the basic responsibilities, you won't have your job long.

(Joe Duffy)

"We can fix the problem in FIVE MINUTES...come back in an HOUR."

FACTOID:

A recent survey of over 3,500 companies showed that 48% test job applicants for drug use; 43% periodically check employees.

Whether you're digging ditches or shouting out stock options, you'd better show up on time.

On Time

Getting to work on time will be one of your most basic responsibilities. Whether you're digging ditches or shouting out stock options, you'd better show up on time. Chapter 7 discusses time management in detail. But for now, just know that if you're in the habit of running late, you'd better shake the habit.

Kelly could work an interview like nobody's business. While all her friends scrambled for jobs their last year of college, Kelly was offered every job for which she interviewed. She had no trouble getting jobs. Keeping them was a different story.

Kelly, now a valued employee of Southwest Airlines, can laugh about the rude awakening of her first job—make that jobs. "I started as a trainee in an investment firm. I'd always been late to my classes. So I thought I was doing great when I came in a couple of minutes late. But they yelled at me. I just thought my supervisor must be mean. So I quit."

The same thing happened to Kelly at her next two jobs. When she landed the job at Southwest Airlines though, she was determined to keep it. "I set my alarm early. I left my apartment early enough to allow for traffic. I'd almost made the first six-month probation period. If you go six months without missing any time or being late, you get a free, reserved air ticket anywhere in the United States. With two weeks to go, my car broke down on the freeway. I was seven minutes late. I didn't get the ticket. But my habit of tardiness was over. I haven't been late in over a year."

HOW TO GET TO WORK ON TIME

1. Set your alarm 30 minutes earlier.

2. Always plan to get to work early—not on time.

3. Use the buddy system with a punctual coworker.

4. Have that second cup of coffee after you get to work.

5. To avoid bad traffic hours, leave an hour early. Use the extra time to get work done, read, or eat breakfast.

6. Set out your clothes (already ironed) the night before.

7. Keep your gas tank filled.

8. Have a Plan B for emergencies—someone who can take you to work, or a cab to call if your car won't start.

9. Never carpool with tardy people.

10. Count on something going wrong and plan accordingly.

Getting the Job Done

Another basic responsibility is simply doing the job. Most jobs aren't like school. You don't put in your time from eight to three and leave as soon as the bell rings.

(V. Harlow/Russell Library)

It's important to complete a job on time because it proves you are a dependable and responsible employee. Prioritize your tasks. Do the hardest part first, and you'll find it easier to finish the entire job.

You don't slide by with minimum effort. At the very least, you hold up your end and get the job done.

Nancy thought of herself as a pretty hard worker when she joined the library staff at a city branch. During her first week, Nancy's boss gave her a list of duties. But instead of taking the list and getting those duties completed, Nancy kept seeing other jobs she could be doing. She wanted to recommend children's books for the library to purchase. She thought of a different way to arrange cassettes.

47

At the end of the week, Nancy was called into the head librarian's office. The library staff was disappointed in Nancy's first week's performance. She hadn't been goofing off. But she failed to get the job done. After that, Nancy made sure she completed every item on her duty list every day.

HOW TO GET THE JOB DONE

1. Do the part you dread first.

2. Mentally move your actual deadline up a week.

3. Make priority lists.

4. Ask questions as soon as you get stuck.

Little Things Mean a Lot

When someone says, "I'll call you," do you expect a call? If somebody borrows your pen, what are the chances you'll get it back? How many times has a friend used something—a book, a T-shirt—and forgotten to return it? When you call a store or business and ask them to return the call, do they?

The truth is, most people don't follow through on the "little things." You can't really count on what they say they'll do, even if you know their intention is good. But if you have a friend who does what he says he'll do, that's a friend you want to keep. That's the kind of a person you can depend on when you need help.

Why not be that kind of person yourself? If you become someone others can count on, you'll be a success no matter what career path you take. How can you do it? Start right now and pay attention to those little things.

The Art of Follow-through

Tara learned the art of follow-through as a child and took the art with her when she was hired as a clerk in a medical clinic. Tara explains, "My mother was a stickler for making us do our chores. If I didn't feed the rabbit, I didn't get an after-school snack. If I told Grandma I'd call her, I'd better do it."

Then Tara was elected to her high school student council. "Before student council, I would have said the only important jobs went to the officers. But after working on committees, I realized it took all of us. They started giving me the jobs that had to get done. So when I started working at the clinic, I was willing to work hard at any job. And my bosses appreciated it. They almost seemed surprised when I'd follow through without anybody making me. Everybody there realizes how important the so-called little things are."

Because Tara proved faithful in the "little things," her bosses began handing over bigger responsibilities. Her follow-through skills earned her a place of leadership in the office.

If you want to make yourself indispensable in your job, follow through with everything. In fact, you can quickly make an impression simply by saying you will do something, then doing it. If you know of a magazine article that might help your bosses or one of your team members, mention it one day and then bring a copy the next day. Be consistent.

Write down the little things in meetings. Someone says, "We need more copy paper." But if you follow through and actually get the paper, you'll probably be the only one. Everybody complains because the office is out of coffee. You can be the only one who thinks of that little need and brings in coffee the next day. Prove how dependable you can be.

▼

You can quickly make an impression simply by saying you will do something, then doing it.

Whoever can be trusted with very little can also be trusted with much.

—Jesus, Luke 16:10

50

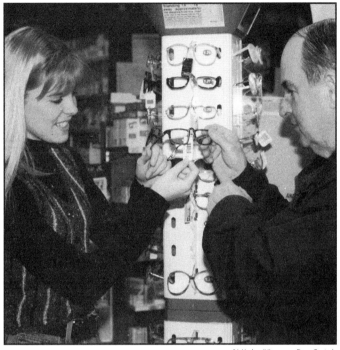

(V. Harlow/Higganum Drug Center)

When working in any sales position, keeping customers happy is a must. Personal, friendly service makes an impression on people and keeps them coming back for more.

Al started working part time in a local Wal-Mart store when he was still in high school. He credits his rapid advancement to his follow-through with customers. Al says, "When a customer comes to me, he wants something. If I don't have exactly what he wants, I have two choices. I can say, 'We don't have it.' Or I can do all I can to follow through and help the customer."

One Christmas, Al drove 40 miles on his own time to get a toy that a customer wanted for her daughter. Then he phoned the customer until he reached her and arranged to meet her at her office so she'd have the gift in time.

You may not have to go quite that far. But you'll have more satisfied customers if you go the extra mile and follow through with your service.

PERSONAL RESPONSIBILITY

Dependability and responsibility begin at home. If you haven't grown up yet, do it now. Take charge of yourself.

Financial Responsibility

Even if you only get a few bucks for a weekly allowance or earn eight dollars for babysitting each week, budget your money. Once you're out on your own—paying for rent, food, entertainment, insurance—you'll have to keep a handle on your finances. If you don't, it will affect your work.

HOW TO EARN A REPUTATION AS SOMEONE TO COUNT ON

1. Get to work early.

2. Stay after hours to get work done.

3. Offer to show a relevant article to a co-worker, then actually deliver it the next day.

4. Remember little preferences (in food or color, etc.) and give people their preference when you have the opportunity.

5. Return borrowed books quickly.

6. If a co-worker shows interest in your resource, give her a copy the next day.

7. Be a detail-oriented person.

8. Take great notes in meetings and refer to them when the meeting stalls.

9. Do the little things nobody wants to (phone calls, legwork, copying).

10. Always beat your deadline.

FACTOID:

Here's how economists suggest allotting monthly income:

housing	30%
utilities	5%
food	20%
medical	5%
personal items	2-4%
clothing	7%
transportation	15%
emergency savings	2%
savings	8%
recreation	4%

—Consumer Credit Counseling Service

Get a simple log to record your spending. Once you see where your money (or your parents' money) is going, you'll know the areas you need to budget. How much can you afford to spend in each area monthly?

One beginning tip is to mark a set of envelopes with the financial category you're budgeting. For example, if you live with your parents, you may only need a few envelopes: Car; Entertainment; Clothes; Gifts and CDs, etc.; Savings; Miscellaneous. Until you get the hang of budgeting, put the actual money allotted into each envelope. Then when the money's

54

gone, you're done. This might keep you from spending everything on movies, for example.

Whatever your system, get a head start on handling your finances. It will be one less worry when you start your career.

Private Responsibility

Another part of your personal responsibility will be keeping your personal life in order. Don't bring your love life dramas to the office.

Try to practice the well-balanced life. Do you have a hobby, something to take your mind off work? Are you in the habit of exercising regularly and eating right? The more lifestyle areas you can get in control now, the better.

TEAM RESPONSIBILITY

Once you become part of a working team, your responsibilities take on an added dimension. You have to become a team player. Each person on a team needs to take personal responsibility for team relationships. You'll have to do more than just be a nice guy. You have to take responsibility for your team's development.

What does it mean to be responsible for team relationships? First, avoid team conflicts. Work for a consensus of agreement. Next, do what you can to draw out quieter team members, to smooth over personality conflicts. Respect and value the other members of your team.

When you become part of a team, your responsibilities shift. Now the team's success becomes more important than your personal success. For example, what would you do if your team voted on Plan B, but you knew beyond a shadow of a doubt that Plan A was better? What if your team met with the entire department to discuss Plan B, and the company boss asked you for your opinion? Where does your responsibility lie? Would you:

As a team player, your first responsibility is to your teammates.

1. Use the opportunity to get your team to change its mind?
2. Tell your boss Plan B isn't your idea?
3. Explain why you believe A is a better plan?
4. Keep your mouth shut?
5. Discuss one or two points you can agree on in Plan B?

Most professionals with team experience would say "5" is the right answer. As a team player, your first responsibility is to your teammates. Express your opinions tactfully and fully in team meetings. But once your team decides on a plan of action, that plan becomes your plan. When the team meeting ends and Plan B is adopted, your responsibility is to help your team with that plan.

PERSONAL INITIATIVE

One of your responsibilities will be to act on your own initiative. Don't always wait until someone tells you what to do. Ask for advice. Learn from the people with experience and expertise. But don't distrust your own abilities. Have the confidence to act on your own and to follow through, without bothering your boss for every little problem.

You run an element of risk when you act on your own. But risk isn't necessarily bad. Few successes come without some element of risk. Do your homework and research. Then don't be afraid to act.

And if you make a mistake, there's one more opportunity to exercise your responsibility. Admit your mistake. Apologize. Don't try to rationalize or excuse your error. Take responsibility and say you're sorry. Then do whatever it takes to try to make up for it.

One general manager, looking back over his career, said, "I've made a lot of mistakes. But in the long run, the mistake itself didn't matter much. It was the way I handled the mistake. That's what made an impression."

Being responsible and dependable is what most employers value more highly than anything else. And it's a quality within your grasp. Go for it!

EXERCISE

1. Name five less-than-responsible things you did last week. Beside each, write what you might have done differently.

2. Draw a pie chart showing how you spend your money. Next, draw a pie chart showing how you'd like to start spending your money. Now, draw up a budget that reflects the second pie chart.

3. Pick one person to convince that you are highly dependable. List 10 "little things" you can do over the next month to prove your point.

CHAPTER FOUR
PROFESSIONAL EXCELLENCE

What if you got a 99% on a science test? Feel pretty good about yourself? Or, say you get 95% on your history mid-term. Not too bad? You'll take it, right?

While 99% or even 95% is usually great on school exams, in the business world it just won't do. You'd better strive for excellence—100%. Here's what would happen if these businesses and agencies settled for 99% instead of 100:

- The IRS would lose 2 million documents this year.
- In the next 60 seconds, 220,000 checks would be deducted from the wrong bank accounts.
- Over 142,000 defective personal computers would be sold this year.
- Approximately 55,172,000 cases of soft drinks would be flat this year.
- Every day, 20 plane landings at O'Hare International Airport in Chicago would crash.

(Courtesy: Chicago Department of Aviation)

In today's fast-paced world, employers expect workers to strive for excellence. Getting it right most of the time just isn't good enough—especially at a place like O'Hare International Airport in Chicago, where thousands of planes take off and land on a daily basis.

- This year, 11,450,000 mismatched pairs of shoes would be shipped.
- About $7,619,000 would be spent this year on tapes and CDs that won't play.
- By the end of the day, 1,070 incorrect medical procedures would be performed.
- *Webster's New International Dictionary* would contain 3,150 misspelled entries.

When you start your career, you raise the stakes. Strive for excellence.

FACTOID:

Office Team, a company that provides temporaries, asked some of the nation's largest companies, "How many typos in a resume does it take for you to decide not to consider a candidate?" Their response: 45% said one typo was enough to eliminate the candidate; 31% said two typos and you're out.

THE WORK ETHIC—THE BELL DOESN'T DISMISS YOU NOW

Excellence isn't an abstract prize which a chosen few can win. Excellence is almost always within your power—if you're willing to work for it. You can always work harder and longer. The bell doesn't dismiss you now.

Marcia recalls what it was like for her to attend her 10th-year high school reunion. Although in high school no one ever noticed her, at the reunion she was a hit—confident and successful.

"I always felt I worked twice as hard for good grades as everybody else had to," Marcia explains. "But I'm glad now. It made me a hard worker on the job. My bosses appreciated how hard I worked. And now, I'm the boss!"

SEVEN SIGNS THAT YOU'RE NOT WORKING HARD ENOUGH

1. Your boss calls you lazy.

2. Your coworkers never want to be assigned to your project.

3. You're bored at the office.

4. You've developed into an excellent Solitaire player on your office computer.

5. Your waste basket is empty.

6. You don't need deodorant.

7. You're fired.

There's a particular pride and satisfaction you get from working hard. You've probably experienced it somewhere—training for an athletic competition, studying extra for a final, finishing an art project after hours of labor.

FACTOID:

The average U.S. high school student spends four hours a week on homework, while youngsters in other industrialized countries average over fours hours a day.

A young man named Popescu came from Romania and took the only job he could get, bagging groceries in a Midwest supermarket. For a couple of years, he worked as hard as he could at his job. And in 1996, Popescu won a grocery bagger competition, to qualify for National Bag-Off, the National Grocers Association's best-bagger contest.

At the competition, the young Romanian was asked by a reporter, "Why do you work so hard at one of the company's lowest-paid positions?"

Popescu grinned and answered, "I'm here to work. What else should I do?" Later, when Popescu was promoted to day stocker, he worked even harder. "When you are raised to a higher position you want to do a better job," he explained. "You want them to think it was right that they put you in that position."

Hold yourself responsible for a higher standard than anybody else expects of you.
                    —**Henry Ward Beecher**

UNSELFISH EXCELLENCE

Hard work and excellence do more than make you look good. You can transform your work team with your professional attitude of unselfish excellence.

Amanda works for a small environmental agency in the Northwest. But she claims she learned the rewards of unselfish excellence in her high school choir. Amanda was usually the soloist for concerts and performances. But in choir, she picked up a valuable lesson. No matter how hard Amanda practiced her solo, the whole choir had to come together. Otherwise, there would be no music—only noise.

Amanda's choir director encouraged small group rehearsals. Choir students learned each other's parts. Amanda helped other sopranos in every way she could. Instead of spending more time on her own part, spending time with her team paid better returns. She opted for team excellence. Their choir achieved beautiful music together, and a first in district competition.

"So that's what I started doing at work," Amanda said. "I looked for ways to help them. And I asked them for help, too. The whole team grew stronger. And I came to appreciate how much everyone else knew." Amanda learned the value of unselfish excellence.

THE PROFESSIONAL

Excellence involves more than hard work. You need to conduct yourself as a professional. Dress, talk and act as a professional.

*If you want to be the CEO, you act like the
CEO. This goes for attitude, dress, hours, and
work ethic.*

—A CEO

PROFESSIONAL DRESS

What should you wear to work? Your best bet is to ask
and observe. Save your rebel streak for after hours
with your old buddies. At work, dress like a professional. This may mean different things in different
work environments, but the safest route is to go con-
servative.

*If you want the job, you have to look the
part. If you want the promotion, you have to
look promotable. If you want respect, you
have to dress as well or better than the
industry standard.*

—Susan Bixler
in *Professional Presence*

Imagine walking into your first job. You only get
one shot at a first impression. What they see is what
they'll think they got. Try not to be the most or least
dressy person there. Business attire usually means

(Joe Duffy)

"You may have a seat over there with the others...and please, don't touch anything."

suits for men and suits, dresses or skirts for women. That's a good place to start. You can always adapt and dress more casually later if you need to.

Don't forget the basics—neat, clean, personal hygiene. The underlying principle of all this is:

Don't let anything get in the way of their discovering how much you have to offer.

Don't let anything get in the way of their discovering how much you have to offer.

DO'S AND DON'TS OF PROFESSIONAL DRESS

Do	Don't
Wear conservative clothes	Be flashy
Wear conservative hairstyle	Wear hair too long, or shave it
Look crisp	Look rumpled
Wear dress shoes	Wear sneakers
Use deodorant/ antiperspirant	Douse perfume
Use make-up sparingly	Use evening make-up
Limit your jewelry	Wear four earings or eight rings

PROFESSIONAL ETIQUETTE

Professional etiquette includes everything from good table manners and environmental awareness to intro-

SELF-DEVELOPMENT SKILLS ▶

ductions and the infamous office Christmas party. Etiquette is a set of rules we live by. Manners are the way we put those rules into effect.

Mind Your Manners

If you don't think manners count in the professional world, listen to Rick's story.

"I joined a production team and felt pretty good about my skills and abilities. My first day, the manager took us out to eat at a fancy restaurant. All of a sudden I felt like a tagalong kid. I didn't know which fork to use. I ordered spareribs, then felt like a cave dweller eating with my hands. I ordered first and got a beer. Nobody else ordered alcohol. I wished I'd listened when my mom used to yell stuff at me during dinner—like 'napkin on lap' and stuff. It was a nightmare."

Don't get caught like poor Rick. Practice good table manners. It's part of being a professional. Be safe when you eat with your coworkers. Don't order anything that will be messy to eat: fried chicken, ribs, spaghetti. Don't order alcohol. Follow other people's lead and don't get the most expensive thing on the menu. And by all means—don't slurp your soup.

TIPS FOR OFFICE LUNCHEONS

1. Don't order "hand food"
   (fried chicken, ribs, spaghetti).

2. Don't salt the peanuts
   (i.e., taste before you salt).

3. Napkin on your lap.

4. No alcohol.

5. Don't order first.

6. Chew with your mouth closed.

7. Take little bites.

8. Don't talk with your mouth full.

9. When more than one fork is at your place
   setting, start with the outside one and
   work your way in.

10. Don't blow your nose at the table.

Greetings

It may sound silly, but don't forget to smile. Everyone in your office deserves a smile and a simple greeting from you. Remember names and titles, too.

Learn how to properly introduce people. For example, say you are introducing your client, Dr. Zhivago, to your coworker, Max Brown. Dr. Zhivago is the one to whom you want to give more respect, and he's the odd-one out, the stranger. Say his name first, and give him the information first:

"Dr. Zhivago, I'd like you to meet our accountant, Max Brown. Max, this is Dr. Zhivago, the client I told you about."

It's a good idea to drop a conversation-starting piece of information to Max: "Max, Dr. Zhivago used to live in your neck of the woods, Chicago." Then they can take it from there.

When you're introduced, pick up on the information if someone has properly introduced you. First, if you're sitting down, stand up. If you're a man meeting a man, extend your hand for a handshake. If you're meeting a woman, it's a courtesy to let her "make the first move," and extend her hand first. If you're the woman, go ahead, let him shake your hand.

FACTOID:

Employees of one construction company attended a seminar on business etiquette to learn, among other things, how to talk to clients on the phone. The chief financial officer reported: "Clients want to hear a smile in your voice. Showing consideration

for and an interest in the caller are the keys
to telephone courtesy."

Environmental Awareness

Most modern offices have taken part in the environmental awareness movement. If you're wasteful, it won't
go unnoticed. Look for a place to recycle your cans and
paper. To cut down on paper cups, bring in your own
mug. Look for ways to cut corners, to reuse, to recycle.

Unspoken After-hours Etiquette

Just because office hours officially end, your professionalism shouldn't. The happily drunk office worker
who dances half naked with a lamp shade on his head
at the office Christmas party may make a funny scene
in an old movie. But it's not professional.

Most work teams are close enough that what happens outside the office has a way of finding its way
into the office. Few secrets survive. As one wise person put it, "Don't do anything you wouldn't want
reported in tomorrow morning's newspaper."

PROFESSIONAL ATTITUDE

It's hard to define, but there's an attitude maintained
by a professional at work. It includes the way you act

toward coworkers, your expectations, what you talk about or bring with you to work and the way you carry yourself.

At home or in high school, you may have grown accustomed to frequent praise as a means of encouragement. Your teacher praised you for working hard. Your mom applauded a good grade. But don't expect that kind of hand-holding from your boss or teammates. They're too busy. Do your job. Be a professional.

Keep an even tone about yourself. Even when the pace gets hectic and anxieties run high, tell yourself, "No drama at work." Speak in a low voice. Take deep breaths, and wait before you react and get pulled into a frenzy. Earn a reputation as someone with a level head.

Professional Privacy

Maybe the best advice on professionalism comes from Lin: "Keep your private life private...and leave your love life at home where it belongs!" After a year working for a Dallas investment firm, Lin learned the hard way how important it was to guard her privacy. "I was going through a break up. Every day I'd come in and spill my heart out. My coworkers listened, but after a while, I felt like nobody took my work seriously. They felt sorry for me and didn't give me a chance at big accounts."

Sharon, on the other hand, is determined not to date anyone from the office and to keep her private life private. She tries to keep "an air of mystery" about herself. When she's at her job in the food industry, she guards her personal privacy. During her first six months at her new job, Sharon broke up with her boyfriend. But she never unloaded her emotions at the office.

Sharon says, "I learned in high school that there were certain girls—and guys—who dump everything. Their love lives were the only things that mattered to them. If they broke up with a boyfriend, you'd see them crying in the halls or running out of class in tears. I would have loved to talk it out with the people I work with. But I didn't want to be one of those girls like I knew in high school. I went to work. I did my job. Then I went home and cried my eyes out on my own time."

PROFESSIONAL HONESTY

You can't have professional excellence without basic honesty. Do you consider yourself an honest person? Most of us do. But the level of professional honesty and integrity has to be high. You have to remain above reproach—so clean, no one will even think you're less than honest.

Customer Honesty

One place for honesty is with your customers. You may be able to push a sale by stretching the claims of your product, but you'll probably lose in the long run. The customer will eventually find out the truth. And you will have lost all the sales he might have brought back. Always go out of your way to play fair, even in the tightest negotiations.

TIPS TO FAIR PLAY WITH CLIENTS

1. Always be up-front. If you don't know, say so.
2. Shoot straight. Don't say "challenge," if you mean "problem."
3. Keep your word. Return calls, and do what you say you will.
4. Treat each client as an individual.
5. Don't make excuses. Take responsibility for errors.

Company Loyalties

You owe loyalty and honesty to your company, too. J. R. Richmond managed Sears and J. C. Penney stores before owning his own department store. He says, "The first thing I demand in an employee is honesty. I had one clerk who charged full for sale items and pocketed the difference. Another I caught in a scam. He'd fill a suitcase with our store items. Then his wife or brother or somebody would come in, and he'd sell them the suitcase."

F A C T O I D :
According to the Fireman's Fund Insurance Company, at least $67 billion are lost each year in the United States to employee cheating and stealing.

WAYS TO BE DISHONEST AT WORK
(almost without realizing it)

1. Pilfer company materials.
2. Punch out at the wrong time.
3. Call in sick, when you're not.
4. Make personal calls on company time.
5. Make numerous personal long-distance calls.
6. Take credit for someone else's idea.
7. Fudge on your expense account.
8. Say you did work, when you didn't.

Everybody's dishonest gain is somebody's loss.
Strive for professional excellence and integrity. Honesty is still the best policy.

EXERCISE

1. Be honest. Name three dishonest things you've done in the past six months. How did you rationalize your dishonesty?

2. Try formally introducing two people this week.

3. Have a quasi-formal dinner during which you try your best to have perfect manners.

4. Plan your wardrobe for the first five days of a new job.

CHAPTER FIVE
5 AGGRESSIVELY NICE

Dian and three of her friends graduated from the same business school. Dian knew two of those friends had better skills than she did. Yet after three years, she was the only one securely on a successful career path. Since they all had worked hard and tried the same businesses, her success remained a mystery to Dian until her boss invited her to lunch.

Dian relates the conversation that gave her insight into her own success. "We finished discussing assignments, and my boss said: 'Dian, you have what it takes to make it.' I asked her what she meant. She said, 'You are *aggressively nice*. Nice won't get it, and neither will aggression. But together, that's a lethal combination.'

"That changed the way I look at myself," Dian continues. "Even in high school on committees, I'd practiced what this woman was telling me. When I was

77

pushy, nobody listened to me. And when I was too nice, nobody paid attention. But aggressively nice worked."

Being aggressively nice means being *thoughtful* and considerate and following through with *thoughtfulness.*

THE POWER OF THOUGHTFULNESS...SIGNED

Kim says she comes by her thoughtfulness honestly. "My mother would sit us down at the kitchen table the day after Christmas. And she wouldn't let us up until we'd written every last thank-you note."

FACTOID:

Franklin D. Roosevelt wrote personal thank-yous to mechanics and acquaintances. He remembered their names and said one of the most important ways of gaining good-will was by making people feel important. Maybe that's why he was elected president four times.

Kim's habit ended up getting her one of her first jobs. "I had my first book accepted for publication by Prentice Hall. I was so excited, until my manuscript came back from the editor. Every line had a correction or suggestion." But instead of despairing, Kim studied each mark until she understood why it read better their way.

"When I was done, I felt I'd had the best editing course in the world. I'd learned so much! So I wrote the editor and told her so. I thanked her. She wrote me back that in her 20 years as an editor, nobody had ever written her a thank-you for editing. When my book was done, that editor offered me a job as a reader for her. Eventually, I did freelance editing for them." Kim's thoughtfulness paid off. If she'd remained silently grateful, that editor never would have known. And Kim wouldn't have gotten a job out of the deal.

MENTORS AND MAILROOMS

It's not just the boss's impression that counts. Be nice to every person you meet. Don't turn off the charm as soon as your boss leaves the room.

Brent works for a city transportation agency in the South. He admits he had to learn the hard way to be nice to everybody. "When I needed something from the mail room, for example, I called down and barked commands. If it didn't get to me fast enough, pity

Don't turn off
the charm as
soon as your boss
leaves the room.

the guy who brought it. Before long, I noticed something odd. I was the last person to get anything from the mail room. I learned my lesson."

Kris Bliss, a public relations specialist in Los Angeles says, "The first person you want to make friends with is the secretary. Nobody has more power or can help you more where it counts. These are people you want to have on your side. And always be friends with the mail room. They know everything."

_____

A great man shows his greatness by the way he treats little men.
**—Thomas Carlyle,
Scottish Essayist and Historian.**

When someone at work does you a favor, say thanks. If a secretary goes out of the way to help you meet your deadline, write a thank-you note. For the receptionist who knows just how to handle those difficult calls, tell him what a great job you think he's doing. Show your appreciation.

AGGRESSIVELY SHOWING THE NICE

How nice are you? You may think you're a nice guy, and you may well be. But if you don't "aggressively" show that niceness, others won't know it. Make five photocopies of the niceness inventory and try it out. (Remember it's not "nice" to mark up a library book!)

Sometimes other people can fill in our blind spots. Trevor never considered himself hard to get to know. But in his senior year in high school he overheard a classmate refer to him as a snob. Trevor didn't feel like a snob, but for the next year he worked on the actions that may have made that impression. He smiled more, made sure he had eye contact when others spoke to him. He tried to show his interest in other people. He was learning to be aggressively nice.

GOLDEN RULE OF INTERPERSONAL SKILLS

Make a list of 10 ways you would like to be treated by team members. Use those principles to help you deal with others. Use the statements below as a guide in developing your list.

- I'd like to be respected.
- I'd like someone to listen when I talk.
- I'd like people to give me the benefit of the doubt.
- I'd like to be appreciated.
- I'd like to be given a chance to show what I can do.

- I'd like to be forgiven when I mess up and not have it constantly thrown in my face.
- I'd like to be congratulated when I do a good job.
- I'd like to be able to trust other people to do what they say they will do.
- I'd like to be left alone when I'm working on a deadline.
- I'd like others to ask me for my opinion.

AGGRESSIVELY NICE IN BUSINESS DEALINGS

What about when you're in the heat of a hostile deal with your competition? What if you're bidding against a competitor or trying to get the lowest price you can get out of your supplier? In times like those, how can a professional still be nice?

Treat every human being as you want to be treated—with understanding, with fairness, with kindness, and with compassion. Give everyone else the same decency and dignity, the same honesty and integrity, the same warmth and concern that you want.
      —Wayne Dosick, *The Business Bible*

HOW NICE ARE YOU?

Circle the number that most fits the way you see yourself. Then ask at least four other people to fill out the assessment as they see you. Include a friend who knows you well, a family member, a teacher and someone who barely knows you. How do the different views of yourself (yours and theirs) compare? How well do you know yourself? Do others perceive you as nice as you believe yourself to be?

	Never	Sometimes	Usually	Always
I smile a lot.	1	2	3	4
I'm friendly to all.	1	2	3	4
I converse easily with peers.	1	2	3	4
I converse easily with elders.	1	2	3	4
I contribute to discussions.	1	2	3	4
I'm easy to talk to.	1	2	3	4
I'm interested in others.	1	2	3	4
I'm respectful.	1	2	3	4
I'm generous.	1	2	3	4
I do my share of the work.	1	2	3	4
I'm dependable.	1	2	3	4
I'm honest.	1	2	3	4
I'm unselfish.	1	2	3	4
I'm polite and courteous.	1	2	3	4
I cooperate with others.	1	2	3	4
I'm an encourager.	1	2	3	4
I return phone calls.	1	2	3	4

Sam Walton created a multimillion-dollar enterprise without losing his friendliness. An officer of one firm that did business with Wal-Mart remarked: "These people [Wal-Mart buyers] are as folksy and down-to-earth as homegrown tomatoes. But when you start dealing with them—when you get past that 'down home in Bentonville' business—they're as hard as nails and every bit as sharp. They'll drive as hard a deal as anyone anywhere."

The oldest business adage is, "The customer is always right."

You don't have to get nasty to make the best deal. Niceness works from a business standpoint. Read mission statements of major corporations. Often, their statements of purpose are ethically and morally oriented, encouraging employees to foster goodwill and help their communities.

Never forget that customers are real people, with needs and families and real frustrations. The oldest business adage is, "The customer is always right." Treat even surly customers with dignity. Try to help them solve their problems. Do your best to empathize with each person. Smile, greet, remember names. People deserve more than, "Next."

YOUR ROLE WITH YOUR TEAM

Even though you're the new kid on the team, you

may be able to play a valuable role in defusing team conflicts. You can be nice to everybody.

But you can take it further—be aggressively nice on your work team. You start out unbiased, free from age-old resentments. Use your position as peacemaker.

You won't like everybody on your team, and that's okay. Some of them may drive you crazy. Your teammates don't need to become your buddies. Respect everybody, like most. Practice empathy. Let people vent around you, without your joining in. You don't have to fix things. Just try to understand. Not everybody will like you either.

You'll be in better shape to be aggressively nice at the office if you meet all the personal needs you can outside the office. Come to work ready to work. Don't lug around a list of needs you expect your teammates to fulfill.

And no matter how nice you are, sooner or later, you'll run into conflict. It may be a personality conflict or a clash of wills. When it happens, be prepared to do whatever it takes to restore harmony. One of the best ways to be aggressively nice in the heat of battle is to apologize.

Never underestimate the power of an apology. You'll be amazed how far the words "I'm sorry" can

> Never underestimate the power of an apology.

take you. Many explosive situations are defused with this formula: Swallow. Take a deep breath. Then say, "You're right. I'm wrong. Sorry."

In most conflicts, both parties are somewhat at fault. Even if the other guy was guiltier than you, you find something to apologize for. And your apology may be all that's needed to restore the peace.

When in doubt, be nice... Aggressively nice.

EXERCISE

1. Make up your own definition of what it means to be "aggressively nice."

2. List three actions you could take today to express your gratitude to someone. Follow through with those actions.

3. When was the last time you apologized to someone or someone apologized to you? What was the effect of the apology?

6

CHAPTER SIX

A LEARNER

Did you know that 89% of knowledge is learned on the job? No wonder many employers believe the number one responsibility of new workers is: to "become learners."

THE POWER OF QUESTIONS

Michael says he owes his relatively smooth transition on his first job to his high school literature teacher. "My teacher made us ask questions. We'd read a story that none of us understood, and he'd make us ask questions until we felt like we knew that story."

Michael took his bag of questions with him and used it from day one when he joined an administrative staff. "I just kept asking questions until I knew my duties and the ins and outs of the company."

(V. Harlow)

When learning a new job, don't hesitate to ask questions. This enables you to learn more quickly what you need to know to perform in the position you were hired for.

One of the most important business skills, particularly in the first few years of entering the real workplace, is the willingness to ask questions and learn as much as possible. There truly is no such thing as a dumb question! Many of the people I started with at my company are mid-level and senior executives because they asked questions of everybody.
—Ann Wolford, problem-solving expert

88

Asking questions can serve several purposes. First, you get answers that equip you to do your job. So ask. Don't be afraid of looking or sounding stupid. It's better to be honest about your ignorance than to pretend you know more than you do because sooner or later, you'll be found out.

Fran just wanted to make a good impression her first day. Her cousin had gone out of his way to get her the job as a typist. But when the supervisor showed Fran where she'd work, Fran realized she'd be doing a lot more than typing.

Fran says, "She asked me if I knew WordPerfect. Before I knew what I was saying, I'd said 'yes.' Then I had to stare at the screen all day because I didn't have a clue. The next day I had to tell the supervisor the truth. I felt about six inches tall crawling into her office."

KEY QUESTIONS TO ASK

1. How exactly does this work?

2. Am I doing this satisfactorily?

3. What could I do to do a better job?

4. Let me see if I understand you correctly.

5. Is there someone I can go to if I need help?

6. How could I help with that?

7. Would you run that by me again?

Besides helping you learn your job, asking questions can get you a reputation as a learner—and that's a reputation you want. There's a world of difference between "I don't know" and "I'd like to know." Don't stop with your lack of knowledge. Make it clear that you really want to know how things work. You want to know all you can about this company. You just can't get enough.

Questions can help you handle conflicts and authority. Put your disagreements in the form of questions. "Do you think it would work to try this?" "What do you think about...?" "If we tried this instead, what do you think might happen?"

Never underestimate the power of a good question.

Rookie-year Learner

Every employee should try to learn as much as possible. But as the new kid in your rookie year on the job, your role as a learner is different from everybody else's.

When Ben joined a group of agricultural extension workers, he brought with him five years of technical education and notebooks full of the latest ideas. His work team had undertaken a county extension project that involved service to farming communities in Iowa. Ben read the plan and knew instantly he had a better idea.

Ben could hardly wait for the first project meeting. As soon as the team leader began reviewing objectives and asking for reports, Ben shared his idea. Instead of the enthusiasm and approval he had expected, Ben's revolutionary plan stirred no interest at all. After the meeting, Ben knew he had done something wrong. He just didn't know what.

Ben forgot his first duty to his work team—to learn. If one of the other members had suggested Ben's plan, it may have received a closer look. Maybe not. Maybe the team already had tried Ben's approach. But Ben was new. The others felt he still had a lot to learn.

LEARNING THE ROPES

Your first year is a learning period. Master your own job. Learn all you can about your company and team members. Some companies appoint new hires a "mentor," a more experienced employee who will show you the ropes. Whether or not your company follows this practice, start looking for your own mentor. (It may or may not be the one you're assigned.)

Another learning practice is the buddy system. Find someone you can ask anything. Make sure it's somebody who likes to answer questions. Be sensitive not to eat up someone else's time. Since we tend to become like the people we spend time with, choose your buddy carefully.

Learn as much as you can about other people's jobs. When you act interested, people consider you interesting. Besides that, with a good knowledge of your team members' responsibilities, you'll be better equipped to help your team. You can pinch-hit when necessary.

When you act interested, people consider you interesting.

EARN YOUR STRIPES

You may think that because you've been hired, you're automatically entitled to the same respect and consideration as everybody else. But you're just a rookie. You have to prove yourself and earn the respect of your team. While you're learning the business your first year, you're laying the foundation for your reputation.

What can you do to earn your stripes? Here are some answers given by team members, from postal workers and department store clerks to business managers and telemarketers.

- *Work harder than anybody else.* Come in early and leave late, even if all you do is polish your desk. Do more than you're asked to do. Develop a reputation as a hard worker.

- *Have a positive attitude* at the office, even if you feel you've made the worst mistake in your life taking this job. Give them a smile and a warm hello.
- *Keep a notebook.* Remember dates, names, clients, instructions. Go home and memorize.
- *Be a professional cheerleader,* quick to congratulate (sincerely) and express appreciation.
- *Be the most available person on your team.* You will probably have more time than established team members. If you get a free minute, ask somebody what you can do to help them. The best thing you have to offer your team is you—your time, your abilities, your energy.
- *Stay sharp, ready for your big moment.* Sarah is an ex-athlete whose high school team skills helped her on her first job. Since she wasn't the best volleyball player on her team, Sarah's main job was cheering from the bench. When the lead was big enough to put her in, she went all out. At her job with an advertising agency, Sarah did what she knew best. She encouraged her team members from the sidelines. And when she got her big moment, a chance to do a presentation for a client, she threw herself into it. And her team cheered for her.

• *Demonstrate your commitment to the company.* Learn all you can about functions and titles and clients. Ask others for their ideas about the future of the business. Do outside research and keep up on competitors. Be knowledgeable. Volunteer for assignments. Ask to sit in on meetings. Join professional organizations. Learn all you can.

TOP RESPONSIBILITIES FOR A LEARNER

1. Ask questions.
2. Learn your job.
3. Learn the jobs of others on your team.
4. Be a "cheerleader" for the team.
5. Learn all you can about your company.
6. Develop good relationships.
7. Work hard.
8. Be available to help where needed.
9. Have a positive attitude.
10. Volunteer for duties.
11. Follow through on every responsibility.

HUMILITY—AN ACCURATE VIEW OF SELF

Good learners have discovered the secret of humility. Humility isn't thinking you're lowly and worthless. It actually means having an accurate picture of yourself—not too high, and not too low.

FACTOID:

The New York Telephone Company made a study of 500 phone conversations to find out the most frequently used word. "I" won—spoken over 3,900 times.

Pride, pretentiousness, and power trips are over-rated. The path to good self-esteem isn't to kid yourself about yourself. Know yourself well, and accept yourself. That's healthy. You can learn what you don't know now anyway.

Don't forget your role as a learner. Earn the respect of your coworkers. Don't demand it. Have a quiet confidence that doesn't have to fake it. Don't be afraid to learn from everyone. Expect even the lowest person on the totem pole to know something valuable you need to learn.

When your head gets too big to fit through
the door, remember where you came from.
Don't rub it in or flaunt it in front of your co-
workers and friends.
                          —**Bradley G. Richardson,**
                Jobsmarts for Twentysomethings

Part of your job is
to make your
boss look good.

Follow

If you have a problem with authority, you better work on it now. Even if your parents allowed constant questioning and your instructor enjoyed your challenges, your boss won't. Save your challenges for the big issues, not the daily demands of your job. Learn how to follow.

How do you follow a boss who seems like an idiot? You salute the uniform. Respect the position. Never try to show her up in public or diminish her authority. Part of your job is to make your boss look good.

A good follower pays attention when other team members talk. No matter how boring, take notes instead of filing or chewing your nails. You may not think anyone notices what you do in meetings, but they do. If you're the only one establishing eye contact with the speaker, you'll be remembered.

Being a follower doesn't mean you keep your

(Joe Duffy)

"Jenkins! As NEW Vice President of the company your FIRST order of business will be to tell the other three you got the promotion!"

mouth shut and sit on your hands. There's a time for everything under the sun—a time to support the ideas of others, a time to contribute your own ideas. Don't feel you have to give your opinion on everything. Pick your spots. Then communicate clearly in as few words as possible. Neither a mouse nor a loudmouth be.

Good followers will become good leaders. But they know that they must first learn to follow.

97

A GOOD FOLLOWER

Makes the boss look good.

Picks his times of disagreement.

Supports team ideas.

Asks for advice.

Gives full attention when others speak.

Follows orders.

Brings solutions, not problems.

A GOOD LEADER

Volunteers for responsibility.

Acts on her own initiative.

Takes input from others and makes decisions.

Contributes in the most helpful way to the team.

Takes personal responsibility for team goals.

Tries to motivate teammates.

Admits when she's wrong.

Is willing to follow others when necessary.

DON'T THINK TOO LOWLY OF YOURSELF

Humility means not thinking too highly of yourself. It also means not thinking too lowly either. Just as you should be realistic about your weaknesses, don't shy away from using your strengths. Know exactly what you have to offer your company that nobody else has.

Just because you're trying to learn as much as possible, don't hold back your talents. Offer them. They may not be snatched up, but you can still make yourself available. Don't pretend to know less than you do. It's all in how you present yourself.

Lead

During your first year, you will probably be more of a follower. But stand ready to lead whenever it helps the team. Leadership means taking responsibility, not credit. Volunteer for jobs that will help your team. Fulfill every responsibility, no matter how small, and your team will come to depend on you.

Leadership means taking responsibility, not credit.

Accept yourself realistically and visualize your own potential. Learn all you can, including what you learn from your own mistakes. Start now to accept yourself so you'll have no need to prove yourself to yourself. Become someone *you* like and trust.

EXERCISE

1. Take an honest look at your last semester in school. List five of the best and five of the worst things about you during that period.

2. Do you tend to think too highly or too lowly about yourself? Explain.

3. Celebrate your successes. List 10 things you did last week that you can feel good about yourself. (For example: completed English assignment, listened to a friend, applied for....)

4. Name three things or processes you'd like to learn this year.

CHAPTER SEVEN
7 MANAGING TIME AND MEMORY

"**W**hat I really need is more time."

"There just aren't enough hours in the day!"

"Where did the time go?"

"She just isn't giving us enough time."

We may complain about time more than anything else. Yet time is one of the few things equally given to everybody on Earth. So, if we're not getting cheated out of the amount of time we get, that just leaves one explanation. We're not managing time well.

THE TYRANNY OF THE URGENT

FACTOID:
Microsoft asked 1,000 businesspeople to identify the most important factor for financial success. Only 32% got the right answer: *having clearly defined goals.*

Cal knew he should have studied for his Spanish quiz last night. But at least he had a study hall before class. He sat down next to the window and started to open his text.

"Cal," Laura said, easing beside him with the grace of a dove. "You have to help me with my algebra."

Cal took one look into Laura's deep brown eyes and knew Spanish could wait long enough to rescue Laura. Ten minutes later Laura closed her algebra book, thanked Cal, and drifted away.

Cal rallied himself. He still had 35 minutes. Plenty of time. He opened to the Spanish vocabulary page, but was interrupted by the PA system: "Anybody trying out for track, meet the coach in the gym for a five-minute briefing."

Cal had to go. It was track, after all. And he'd still have time when he got back. But when he got back to study hall 10 minutes later, he had to make a pit stop at the men's room. In study hall a note from his girlfriend was waiting for him. Somebody had gotten word to her that he'd been flirting with the fair Laura. He *had* to straighten out that misunderstanding.

As Cal sidled over to his girlfriend's table, he was stopped by the art teacher—something about cleaning up his mess in the art room...now! As Cal wiped the last dried glob of red paint from the art room chalkboard, the bell rang. Time for Spanish.

Cal was suffering from "the tyranny of the urgent." Some of us live our lives without a plan, bouncing from one urgency to another. In the business world, you're going to have times of hectic pace, urgencies that demand your attention. Your job is to stay in control.

Have you ever watched people ski? Beginners tumble at the mercy of the hill. The novice controls his descent by fighting the hill, braking all the way. But the expert skier goes with the hill, controlling his own movement. He's not afraid to run out of control. He enjoys the speed of the hill, because he knows he can resume control when he needs too.

That's what you need to do in the fast-lane business world. Enjoy the ride and go with it when you want to. But know that you can pull out when you need to. Otherwise, you'll go down in the drift of things that have to get done this minute. You'll never get to important-but-not-urgent. And you'll hate the ride.

To keep your head up out there: 1. Get your priorities straight. 2. Set personal goals. 3. Plan and schedule.

GET YOUR PRIORITIES STRAIGHT

Start by listing the things that are most important to you. Your buddies or the love of your life? Your family? Playing the guitar or drums or becoming a concert pianist? Getting a job this summer? Losing 15 pounds? Making lots of money? Making good grades? Being popular?

Brainstorm a list of your priorities. Then arrange your list in order, with the most important things near the top. Now you have something to work with and form into goals.

SETTING PERSONAL GOALS

Haven't you noticed that if you don't plan things, they don't get done? You may really want to learn the guitar. But until you transform that desire, that priority, into a workable goal, you'll be singing a cappella.

Goals come in all sizes, from life goals to daily goals. If you've never set goals before, it might be worth your time to jot down a general, life goal in each major area of your life:

- Family
- Financial
- Intellectual
- Physical
- Social
- Spiritual
- Vocational
- Other

For example, a long-range social goal might be: "To be at ease and functional in every kind of social situation." A long-range financial goal might be: "To be debt free, with enough money to buy the necessities and be free from money worries." Or, "To be a billionaire."

_____

Goals define our mission in life. Without goals, we have no criteria to judge each job or career change.

**—Amy Lindgren,
President of Prototype Career Services**

Short-term Goals

But your goals will have to get specific if they're going to help you. You need to set short-term goals. Try setting up goals for one semester. Now you get to chip away at a piece of that life goal.

For example, realistic financial goals for this semester might be:
- "Get a part-time job."
- "Save $200 this semester."
- "Pay my brother back his $75."

Other goals for the semester might include:
- Raise my geometry grade one letter.
- Pass chemistry.

105

- Make the honor roll.
- Be on time to class every day.
- Keep my locker organized.
- Get a role in the play.
- Get along with Coach.

Short-term Goal Ideas

Your next step is to break up your goals into parts or steps, called objectives. If you fulfill each objective, you'll reach your goal. For instance, decide on several steps to save $200 by the end of the semester. You'll take the job flipping burgers after school. You'll put aside $30 each week and deposit it in the bank.

Do this with each goal, breaking it down into manageable steps. Now you have your plan.

SCHEDULE THE PLAN

So far you have goals, objectives and plans. But what you need to do is work with the time you've got. Say you've made it your goal to study for tests this semester. But what you'll have to do to make it happen is schedule it in. Make yourself a weekly schedule.

Now, schedule, schedule, schedule. Write in the givens: school, work hours, sleep, Saturday Night Live. Then schedule in activities you've worked out in your short-term goals. If you study from 7 to 9 Monday and Tuesday nights, you know you'll have time to prep for tests. Look at your syllabi and plan extra study nights for scheduled exams.

Write in your exercise times and when you'll weigh in to see how you're doing. And don't forget to schedule in fun.

WEEKLY PLANNER

Time	Mon.	Tues.	Wed.	Thurs.	Fri.	Sat.	Sun.
7:00 A.M.							
8:00 A.M.							
9:00 A.M.							
10:00 A.M.							
11:00 A.M.							
12:00 P.M.							
1:00 P.M.							
2:00 P.M.							
3:00 P.M.							
4:00 P.M.							
5:00 P.M.							
6:00 P.M.							
7:00 P.M.							
8:00 P.M.							
9:00 P.M.							
10:00 P.M.							
11:00 P.M.							

Guard well your spare moments. They are
like uncut diamonds. Discard them and their
value will never be known.
                    —Ralph Waldo Emerson

Do it!

You have goals, objectives, a plan, and a schedule. Now all you have to do is do it! And the only thing that can get in your way is you.

Beware of procrastination—the habit of putting off until tomorrow...and the next day...and the day after.... It's a habit you'd better break.

Although there's no proven cure for procrastinators, keep in mind the tips in the box on page 110.

MEMORY SKILLS

Just as with a little work and planning you can manage your time, you can learn to manage your memory. And if you want to excel in business, a good memory can be an incredible asset.

David learned the hard way. In his first month in telemarketing, he called his boss by the wrong name, forgot where he put his employee manual, spaced out during an early morning meeting and forgot an important client's identity. Bad enough, but there was more.

(Courtesy: Prints & Photographs Division, Library of Congress)

Being able to plan and follow a schedule is the key to having an organized life. American philosopher Ralph Waldo Emerson urged people to value and use their spare time wisely.

David explains: "I knew I was supposed to ship to Indiana, the city—Indiana, Pennsylvania. But it slipped my mind. I shipped a huge order to the state of Indiana. That was the last straw. I knew I needed to improve my memory."

David read a book, practiced and improved his memory. Generally, memory consists of three elements: acquiring, storing, and recalling. Most of us have our biggest problems with recall. There are

HOW TO STOP PROCRASTINATING

1. Find out where you're wasting your time.

2. If fear of failure is holding you back, admit it.

3. Make yourself accountable to another person. ("I will start my exercise program this Saturday. My goal is to lose one pound this week.")

4. Is your problem starting a project? Schedule an exact time to begin.

5. Is your problem finishing? Set up a system of checks and balances. (A chart where you write down your weight every Friday; a joint work session when you'll have to show someone how much you've done.)

6. Break the big picture into less-threatening steps.

7. Reward yourself at various stages. (If you read 50 pages, you get a bowl of ice cream—unless, of course, you're also trying to lose weight!)

8. Celebrate the little victories along the way.

9. Get a partner, someone with a similar goal.

10. Give your goal a reality check. If you've never run a mile, you're probably shooting too high to enter the marathon.

many techniques out there to help you manage your memory. We'll take a look at a few of the simplest.

Listen Up

Probably the simplest memory aid is to improve your listening. Pay attention when someone gives you her name. When you're about to receive an important piece of information, stop what you're doing and give your full attention. If you're not sure you understand, ask to have it repeated.

Write It Down

Make use of lists and calendars. Use a personal organizer. Write down meeting times and dates. Check your calendar every day. If you have a good organizational system, you won't have to remember so much.

Make lists. If you're supposed to remember to file a report, drop off some papers, pick up supplies, jot it on your today's "to do" list. But don't forget to look at it.

Association

Say you want to remember your shopping list: eggs, butter, garlic, spaghetti, and dog food. Try to make an unforgettable association with the words: You're using a stick of butter as a skateboard, racing down the sidewalk, your dog barking along behind. Your hair has turned to spaghetti, streaming in the wind. You hold a raw egg in each outstretched arm. And passersby cross the street because of your garlic breath. Now, there's a picture that's harder to forget than your original list. And you should be able to pick out the items you need. You've associated them.

Visualization

If you can picture what you want to remember, you'll have a better chance at remembering it. Imagine Ms. Leopard in a leopard-skin coat; Mr. Brown dressed totally in brown; Ms. Cratchet with a ratchet. The more offbeat the image, the easier it is to remember.

FACTOID:
According to psychologists, a "short-term memory" is a working memory capable of recording seven items for a maximum of 30 seconds. An example is holding a phone number in your mind long enough to dial it.

Mnemonics

Mnemonics are tricks to help you remember. You could use alliteration (mean Mrs. Masters made me mad). Or, simple repetition or rhyme could help your memory: "Use legs, get eggs."

Acronyms are made-up words or groups of letters to help you remember several items starting with those letters. BEAT=butter, eggs, apple, toast. HOMES=Huron, Ontario, Michigan, Erie, Superior (the Great Lakes).

You can make up your own code to help you spell a name correctly: Treit=That rat eats ice, too. Or, memorize the names and order of the planets by making up a sentence using words that begin with the same first letters as planet names: My (Mercury) very (Venus) elderly (Earth) mother (Mars) just (Jupiter) served (Saturn) us (Uranus) nine (Neptune) pizzas (Pluto).

Manage your memory and manage your time, and you'll be way ahead of the game when you start your new career.

TIPS FOR REMEMBERING NAMES

1. Pay attention!

2. Repeat the name aloud.

3. Write it down when the person leaves.

4. Make a rhyme: Matt Spry = Fat Guy.

5. Make up a visual image of the person connected with his name: Mr. Mallard riding a duck.

6. Make an acrostic of the name: Mrs. Hales = Horrible Aliens Let Eagles Sing.

EXERCISE

1. Keep a time chart of what you do throughout one day. Include everything: "3:05 to 4:10 Talked with friends; 4:10 to 5:30 Watched TV...."

2. Develop a pie chart that reflects how you use your time.

3. List your top five time wasters.

4. Decide on one thing you want to accomplish tomorrow, something you just haven't seemed to be able to get done. Now, draw up a schedule and schedule in that activity. Do it.

5. Without using any memory "tricks," see how many items you can memorize on this list: turkey, ring, car, tomato, basket, cheese, pencil. Give yourself five minutes to read the list and commit it to memory. (Remember, no tricks.)

   Do something else for 5 minutes. Then see how many you remember. Wait 20 minutes and try again.

   Finally, make up a mental picture, a visual that includes all the items (a turkey carrying a basket...). Give yourself a memory check after 5 minutes and after 20 minutes. You should be able to remember all the items now.

CHAPTER EIGHT
8 WORK YOUR HEART OUT... BUT TAKE IT EASY

Ever notice how life is filled with opposites? Relax, but be on your guard. Trust people, but watch your back. Be nice, but don't let them walk all over you. Live for the moment, but plan for the future. Have confidence that you can do anything, but be realistic about your limitations.

That's life. It's a balance. This book has covered a lot of areas you can work on to get ready for a great career. But none of it will do you much good if you're too stressed out on the job to enjoy your life.

So, we'll close with some hot tips provided by people who learned about stress and self-esteem on the job. The material that follows comes from interviews with first- and second-year employees in a wide range of careers and positions—from investors to truckers, airline flight attendants to news reporters.

UNREASONABLE EXPECTATIONS

FACTOID:

In 1995, the average starting salary for college grads was $24,000. The average salary for males between 25 to 34 is only $26,197; for females $21,510.—*Newsweek*

Get real. You're not going to come in like a Broadway play and wow the corporation your first week. You probably won't get a raise your first year. Nobody will pat you on the back for coming in on time and doing what they hired you to do. Your first employee evaluation will be lukewarm.

When you come in with too many unreasonable expectations, you set yourself up for stress and disappointment. Remember, your first year is a time to learn. Let them teach you. Be a sponge. Have fun getting smart. You can wow them later.

Be Prepared

Those Boy Scouts know what they're talking about. Being brave has a lot to do with being prepared. Andrew pulled As and Bs in high school and college with little effort. He says, "I could always wing it when I had to give a speech or report."

Then he got his job with a research team in California. "The first time I had to present findings, I tried to wing it. I got so nervous the morning of our meeting, I could barely talk."

Don't "wing it" on the job. Prepare. Overprepare until you don't have to think about what you'll say. Solid preparation is one of the surest ways to relieve job stress. Take the pressure off.

Solid preparation is one of the surest ways to relieve job stress. Take the pressure off.

TOP CAUSES OF JOB STRESS

1. Unreasonable job expectations
2. Lack of preparation
3. Financial problems
4. Lack of self-forgiveness
5. Inability to flex
6. Unhappiness outside the office
7. Personality clash
8. Lack of job knowledge or skill
9. No outside interest or life
10. Poor self-image
11. Not enough sleep

THE POWER OF DOING YOUR DARNDEST

You might think you'll have a better chance of escaping job stress if you don't work so hard. But usually,

117

the opposite is true. There's a kind of power in doing your darndest.

When you work hard and do your best, you don't have to kick yourself when something goes wrong. You can at least know that you did what you could. And others will know it, too.

If you have to be at work for eight hours, you might as well work hard. Then you can play hard when you get home.

Make a name for yourself as someone who can fill in almost anywhere.

ROLLING WITH THE PUNCHES

Don't forget that nobody can predict the future. Your job will probably not be what you expected. And just when you get the hang of it, it will change. You have to change with it.

Learn to flex. If you stubbornly resist change or show your resentment every time you have to shift directions, you'll be considered hard to work with. Relax. Flex. You can't stop the changes, so you might as well be a good sport. Besides, you're bucking for a promotion. Your job will change then anyway.

The more you learn about your job and everybody else's job, the better. Ask questions. Be versatile. Make a name for yourself as someone who can fill in almost anywhere. Then, if your company downsizes and lays

118

people off, you'll be someone they can't afford to let go. If they phase out your position, they know you'll fit in anywhere.

MARK YOUR SUCCESSES

Most of us pay a lot more attention to our failures than to our successes. But if you want to build your self-esteem, give yourself credit for the little successes along the way.

If you get to work early every day for a week, and that's an accomplishment for you, pat yourself on the back. You deserve credit. If you know you did your best and did more than was required of you that day, then good for you. Celebrate your success. If you keep a journal, write down your victories.

WHEN YOU BLOW IT

Job stress is usually at its highest when you make a mistake. Everybody will make mistakes on the job. How you handle your mistakes will determine your level of stress.

First, try to keep a positive perspective. Put the mistake in light of all the things you've done right. Don't keep focusing on it and interpreting everything around you in light of that error. It's just a small part of a much bigger picture.

(V. Harlow)

Balance your life between work and play. Having a hobby helps take your mind off work, and gives you something to look forward to so you can relax and recharge your batteries after a hard week's work.

There may be no better teacher than to make a mistake and learn from it.

Own up when you blow it. Don't try to shift the blame. Don't waste time trying to explain yourself and justify the mistake. Do what you need to do. Admit it. Apologize. Try to lessen the fallout.

Forgive yourself first. If you don't, the mistake will stick with you, making you afraid to take the necessary risks of your job. You can paralyze yourself with indecision. Instead, accept it and move on. You're okay, and just as smart as you were before you blew it.

120

Learn from your mistakes. There may be no better teacher than to make a mistake and learn from it. So don't waste a golden opportunity by reveling in self-pity.

A SENSE OF HUMOR

Finally, learn to laugh at yourself. Over and over, men and women reported that a healthy sense of humor is the best stress reliever.

Find the humor in every stressful situation. And make sure that humor is directed at you, and not at someone else. A good sense of humor can restore perspective, defuse tense negotiations, and patch up bruised relationships.

Fill Up at Home

The balanced career person has a life outside the workplace. Keep your home life in order, a place of refuge. Have a hobby you can pull out to distract yourself. Give yourself outside events and engagements to look forward to, especially when you're not looking forward to going in to work. Take care of yourself with healthy eating, ample sleep, and regular exercise.

NEEDS YOUR JOB PROBABLY WON'T FULFILL

1. Your lovelife

2. Your need for a best friend

3. Exercise

4. Fun

5. Spiritual fulfillment

6. Relaxation

7. Emotional release

Don't try to get all your needs fulfilled through your work. Your life is more than what you do. Start now to work on your self-development. Become the kind of person you'd hire if you were the boss. Become the kind of person you'd like to be.

GLOSSARY

Acronyms. Made-up words or groups of letters to help us remember several items starting with those letters.

Aggressively nice. Thoughtful and considerate, acting and following through on the thoughtfulness.

Choleric. One of the four temperaments: confident, usually goal-oriented and capable.

Ethics. A system of morals; the code of unwritten rules about how we act toward others.

Etiquette. The unwritten rules of good manners and taste.

Extrovert. Outgoing; usually people who enjoy and are at ease in crowds and in new situations.

Humility. Thinking accurately about oneself—not too highly, and not too lowly.

Initiative. The act of taking the first step or making the first move.

Introvert. The tendency to keep to oneself, rather than seeking other people.

Learning Style. An individual's preferred method for acquiring information.

Melancholy. One of the four temperaments: artistic, usually organized and analytical, sensitive.

Mentor. An unofficial teacher, coach, advisor.

Mnemonics. An aid to recall things through rhyme, alliteration, repetition, etc.

Phlegmatic. One of the four temperaments: generally easy going, well-balanced, steady.

Procrastination. The act of putting tasks off until "tomorrow".

Sanguine. One of the four temperaments: outgoing, life of the party, popular.

Temperament. One's nature, or customary frame of mind and natural disposition.

Values. The things and principles most important to us.

Work Ethic. A system of values where much importance is ascribed to working hard.

BIBLIOGRAPHY

Brallier, Lynn. *Successfully Managing Stress.* Los Altos, Calif.: NNR, 1982.

Dosick, Wayne. *The Business Bible: Ten New Commandments for Creating an Ethical Workplace.* New York: HarperCollins Business Books, 1994.

Frey, Diane and C. Jesse Carlock. *Enhancing Self Esteem.* Muncie, Ind.: Accelerated Development Inc., 1984.

Harrison, Allen F. and Robert M. Bramson, Ph.D. *Styles of Thinking: Strategies for Asking Questions, Making Decisions, and Solving Problems.* New York: Anchor Press/Doubleday, 1982.

Kinlaw, Dennis C. *Developing Superior Work Teams.* Lexington, Mass.: Lexington Books, D.C. Heath and Company, 1991.

LaHaye, Tim F. *Spirit-Controlled Temperament.* Wheaton, Ill.: Tyndale House Publishers, 1967.

Lapp, Danielle C. *(Nearly) Total Recall.* Stanford, Calif.: Stanford Alumni Association, 1992.

Lorayne, Harry. *How to Develop a Super Power Memory.* Hollywood, Fla.: Fell Publishers, Inc., 1989.

McCormack, Mark H. *The 100% Solution.* New York: Villard Books, 1990.

Richardson, Bradley G. *Jobsmarts for Twentysome-things.* New York: Vintage Books, Random House, 1995.

Simon, Sidney B., Leland W. Howe, and Howard Kirschenbaum. *Values Clarification: A Handbook of Practical Strategies for Teachers and Students.* New York: Dodd, Mead, & Co., 1992.

Terkel, Susan Neiburg. *Ethics.* New York: Lodestar Books, E.P. Dutton, 1992.

Vance, Sandra S. and Roy V. Scott. *WalMart: A History of Sam Walton's Retail Phenomenon.* New York: Twayne Publishers, 1994.

Wainwright, Gordon. *Essential Personal Skills for Life and Work.* San Diego, Calif.: Pfeiffer & Company, 1993.

A

actions 34
aggressively nice 77-86
agreement, consensus of 56
alone-time 23
apology 85-86
attire, business 65-66
attitude, positive 93
awareness, environmental 67, 71

B

balance, in life & job 115
brain hemisphere dominance (list) 20
brain, functioning of: left-brain 19-20, 21; right-brain 19, 21
brainstorm 104
buddy system (on job) 91-92

C

character 7, 9, 10
cheerleader, professional 93, 94
commitment 94
conflict(s) 86, 90; defusing team 85; ethical 35-36; personality 85; team 56
control (on job)
creativity 37

D

decisions 34
dependability (on the job) 43-58
dictator 18
disagreement(s) 90

E

Emerson, Ralph Waldo 108, 109
ethical dilemma 36
ethics, 25, 35-40; code of 39-40
excellence: team 64; unselfish 63-64
expectations, unreasonable (on job) 116-117
experience 7
extroverts 21-22
eye contact 81, 96

F

follow, how to (on job) 96-97
follower 96-97, 99; traits of 98

follow-through 17, 48-52; art of 49-52; skills 50

G

getting job done, how to 48
go-ahead kick 12
goal-oriented 18
goals 34; daily 104; financial 105; life 104; personal 103, 104-106; short-term 105-106, 107; social 104

H

home life 121
honesty 27, 37
how nice are you, an assessment 82
humility (on job) 95-97, 99
humor (on job) 121

I

initiative, personal 57-58
integrity 34-35, 37, 74
introverts 21-22

K

knowledge 87
know yourself 12

L

laziness 16
leader, traits of 98
leadership 99
learner 87-99; auditory 20, 21; kinesthetic 20, 21; responsibilities of on job (list) 94; visual 20, 21
learning styles 18-20; applying knowledge of 21-22
life, personal 55

M

manners, table 67
memory aids: association 111-112; listening 111; lists & calendar 111; mnemonics 112-113; visualization 112;
mentor (on job) 79, 91
Meyer-Briggs Type Indicator (personality inventory) 13
mistake(s) (on job) 119

127